AMAZING SIGHTS IN THE SKY
ECLIPSES

by Jane P. Gardner

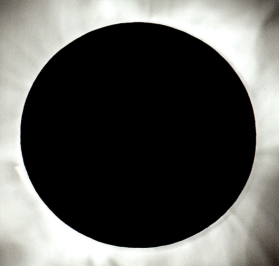

Ideas for Parents and Teachers

Pogo Books let children practice reading informational text while introducing them to nonfiction features such as headings, labels, sidebars, maps, and diagrams, as well as a table of contents, glossary, and index.

Carefully leveled text with a strong photo match offers early fluent readers the support they need to succeed.

Before Reading

- "Walk" through the book and point out the various nonfiction features. Ask the student what purpose each feature serves.
- Look at the glossary together. Read and discuss the words.

Read the Book

- Have the child read the book independently.
- Invite him or her to list questions that arise from reading.

After Reading

- Discuss the child's questions. Talk about how he or she might find answers to those questions.
- Prompt the child to think more. Ask: Have you viewed an eclipse? Would you like to?

Pogo Books are published by Jump!
5357 Penn Avenue South
Minneapolis, MN 55419
www.jumplibrary.com

Copyright © 2021 Jump!
International copyright reserved in all countries. No part of this book may be reproduced in any form without written permission from the publisher.

Library of Congress Cataloging-in-Publication Data

Names: Gardner, Jane P., author.
Title: Eclipses / by Jane P. Gardner.
Description: Minneapolis: Jump!, Inc., [2021]
Series: Amazing sights in the sky | Includes index.
Audience: Ages 7–10 | Audience: Grades 2–3
Identifiers: LCCN 2019058945 (print)
LCCN 2019058946 (ebook)
ISBN 9781645275626 (hardcover)
ISBN 9781645275633 (paperback)
ISBN 9781645275640 (ebook)
Subjects: LCSH: Eclipses—Juvenile literature.
Classification: LCC QB175 .G37 2021 (print)
LCC QB175 (ebook) | DDC 523.3/8—dc23
LC record available at https://lccn.loc.gov/2019058945
LC ebook record available at https://lccn.loc.gov/2019058946

Editor: Jenna Gleisner
Designer: Molly Ballanger

Photo Credits: muratart/Shutterstock, cover; Vadim Petrakov/Shutterstock, 1; JNix/Shutterstock, 3; Herrieynaha/Shutterstock, 4; thePDXphotographer/ Shutterstock, 5; Aphelleon/Shutterstock, 6-7; Baranov E/Shutterstock, 8-9; Miloslav Druckmuller/SuperStock, 10-11; VaLiza/Shutterstock, 12-13 (girl); underworld/ Shutterstock, 12-13 (moon); Lukasz Pawel Szczepankshi/ Shutterstock, 14-15; Igor Shoshin/Shutterstock, 16-17; Pixel-Shot/Shutterstock, 18; Allexxandar/Shutterstock, 19; Mohammef Abubakr/EyeEm/Getty, 20-21; NASA Images/Shutterstock, 23.

Printed in the United States of America at Corporate Graphics in North Mankato, Minnesota.

TABLE OF CONTENTS

CHAPTER 1
Solar Eclipses 4

CHAPTER 2
Lunar Eclipses 12

CHAPTER 3
Viewing Eclipses 18

ACTIVITIES & TOOLS
Try This! 22
Glossary 23
Index 24
To Learn More 24

CHAPTER 1
SOLAR ECLIPSES

August 21, 2017, was an exciting day. People waited to view a major event. They wore special sunglasses to protect their eyes. Why?

There was a **total solar eclipse** that day. People across the United States watched. The sun appeared smaller. Then it vanished!

CHAPTER 1

What causes a **solar eclipse**? The Earth, moon, and sun travel along paths in space. These are called **orbits**. Earth orbits the sun. The moon orbits Earth. When their orbits line up, an eclipse occurs. The moon moves directly between Earth and the sun. The moon casts a shadow on Earth.

DID YOU KNOW?

Solar eclipses are not rare. The sun, Earth, and moon line up often! This happens about once every 18 months.

CHAPTER 1

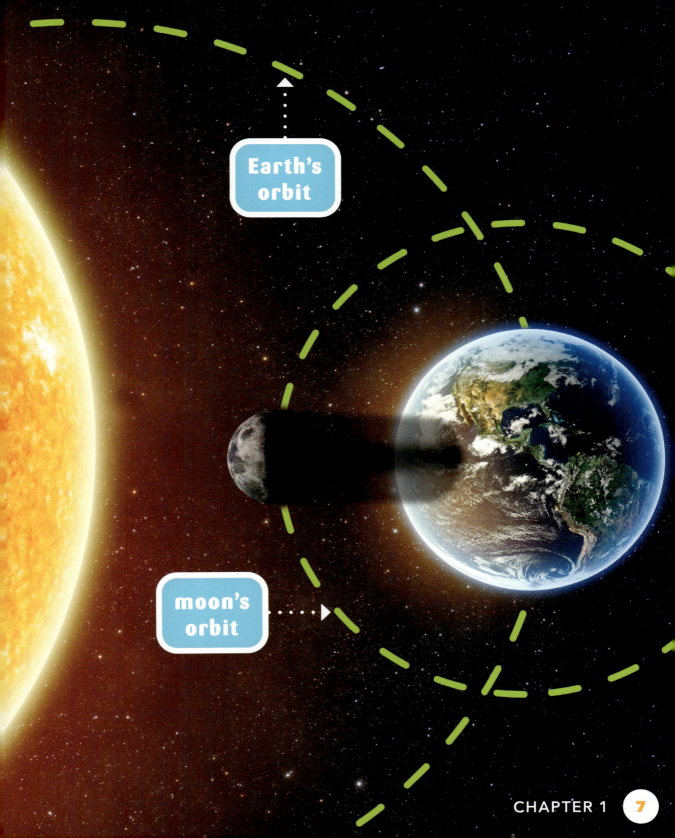

CHAPTER 1

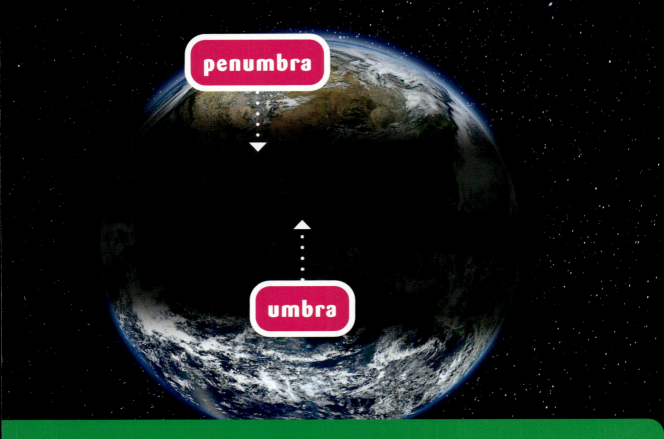

The shadow made by the moon is called the **umbra**. People in the path of the umbra see a total solar eclipse. The sun is completely blocked from view. It is very dark.

Around the umbra is a lighter shadow. This is the **penumbra**. People in the penumbra see a **partial eclipse**. Parts of the sun are still visible.

CHAPTER 1

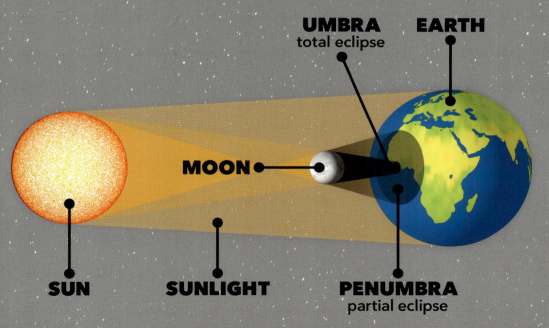

corona

CHAPTER 1

During a total eclipse, you can still see the sun's **corona**. Why? This ring of light is part of the sun's **atmosphere**. It is usually hidden by the sun's bright light!

DID YOU KNOW?

Total solar eclipses don't last long. Why? The moon is moving along its orbit. The 2017 eclipse lasted longest in Tennessee. It only lasted two minutes and 40 seconds.

CHAPTER 1   11

CHAPTER 2
LUNAR ECLIPSES

Lunar eclipses happen, too. These happen when Earth comes between the moon and the sun. Earth casts a shadow on the moon.

Usually, the moon looks white. Why? Sunlight **reflects** off the moon's surface.

During a lunar eclipse, the sun's rays **refract**, or bend, around Earth. The light looks different. The moon looks red!

CHAPTER 2

partial lunar eclipse

16 CHAPTER 2

Partial lunar eclipses happen, too. How? Only part of the moon passes through Earth's shadow. During partial lunar eclipses, part of the moon seems to disappear!

DID YOU KNOW?

Eclipses are visible from the moon, too! During one, Earth is ringed in red light.

CHAPTER 2   17

CHAPTER 3

VIEWING ECLIPSES

Lunar eclipses are safe to view. Just look up at night! You can use a telescope to view them, too.

If you want to watch a solar eclipse, have a **solar filter** or viewer ready. Why? The sun's rays are very strong. They can damage your eyes.

solar filter

CHAPTER 3

Do you know when the next solar or lunar eclipse will be? Research to find out! There are many amazing sights to see in the sky!

CHAPTER 3

ACTIVITIES & TOOLS

TRY THIS!

MAKE YOUR OWN ECLIPSE

Shadows create eclipses. Try making your own eclipse!

What You Need:
- a dark room
- a few friends
- a flashlight
- a large round object, such as a globe or basketball
- a small round object, such as an orange or baseball

❶ Darken a room.

❷ Have one friend turn on the flashlight. That person is acting as the sun. He or she will not move.

❸ Have another friend hold the larger round object out at arm's length. This person is acting as Earth. Place or hold Earth in one position.

❹ Have another friend hold the smaller round object out. This person is acting as the moon. Hold the moon in different spots. See what shadows it makes as it passes between the sun and Earth.

❺ What shadows form when Earth comes between the moon and the sun?

GLOSSARY

atmosphere: The mixture of gases that surrounds a planet or celestial body.

corona: The outermost part of the sun's atmosphere.

lunar eclipses: Eclipses in which the moon appears darkened as it passes into Earth's shadow.

orbits: The curved paths the moon, planets, and other satellites take as they circle another planet or the sun.

partial eclipse: An eclipse in which only part of a celestial body is obscured or darkened.

penumbra: The partially shaded outer region of the shadow during an eclipse.

reflects: Throws back light from a surface.

refract: To bend.

solar eclipse: An eclipse in which the sun is blocked from view by the moon.

solar filter: A tool that blocks most of the sunlight to avoid damage to the eyes.

total solar eclipse: An eclipse in which the sun, moon, and Earth are in a direct line.

umbra: The fully shaded inner region of the shadow during an eclipse.

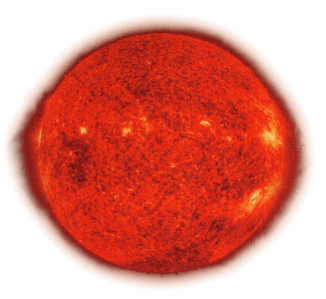

ACTIVITIES & TOOLS

INDEX

atmosphere 11
corona 11
Earth 6, 9, 13, 14, 17
eyes 4, 19
lunar eclipses 13, 14, 18, 20
moon 6, 8, 9, 11, 13, 14, 17
orbits 6, 11
partial eclipse 8, 9, 17
penumbra 8, 9
shadow 6, 8, 9, 13, 17

solar eclipse 5, 6, 8, 9, 11, 19, 20
solar filter 19
sun 5, 6, 8, 9, 11, 13, 14, 19
sunglasses 4
sunlight 9, 14
telescope 18
total solar eclipse 5, 8, 9, 11
umbra 8, 9
view 4, 8, 18
viewer 19

TO LEARN MORE

Finding more information is as easy as 1, 2, 3.

1. Go to www.factsurfer.com
2. Enter "eclipses" into the search box.
3. Click the "Surf" button to see a list of websites.

24 ACTIVITIES & TOOLS